Passionate Insights in Rhyme

Passionate Insights in Rhyme

Amalia Jusayan

Copyright © 2022 Amalia Jusayan

asj5132@aol.com

ISBN 978-0-578-39121-2

Edited and designed by Tell Tell Poetry

Printed in the United States of America

First Printing, 2022

For my dearest departed parents, Gil and Magdalena, and for my brothers and sisters and their respective families, whom I have kept close to my heart regardless of time and distance.

For my friends and brethren in faith, who were always there to share their love and extend their support in my down times and when I needed them the most.

For Kallie, who has been around always at any given moment, inspiring and guiding me most patiently, and who has invested her invaluable time to help make my cherished dream of an awesome and magnificent book of poetry into a glaring reality!

Most of all for God Almighty, for the talent He has gifted me with that enabled me to express my insights through poetry. Into His hands I totally entrust the success of this wonderful and amazing creation.

Contents

Acknowledgments

Thank you to the Tell Tell Poetry team for all their invaluable help with editing, designing, and publishing this book.

Passionate Insights in Rhyme

Soul Rejuvenated

My heart once magically caved in
to the wondrous feeling we call love,
unaware of everything around me
except for things only hearts can see.

Truth naturally happens,
staring us in the eye long before time,
the brain above the heart written in books—
awesome creations, amazing handiwork.

Though wisdom is hidden in plain sight,
it guides us to do what is right.
Absent wisdom, desire fogs reason.
Humanity fell due to desires of the heart.

Hence we need to objectively see things,
think through all consequences,
find Lady Wisdom deep within.
Righteous acts will spark a delight of being.

All of life's moments are worth reckoning
with a pristine desire to live in peace.
Life's akin to a roller coaster ride—
ups and downs spell the truth of being alive.

Life's ups and downs define the true essence
of what this crazy world really is all about.
What would it be like if life's rhythm were flat,
so devoid of meaning and putting up a fight?

But man's resolve weakens against temptation
to the nonsensical. He crazily compromises.
Crazy fights cause loss of lives.
We must stay calm and embrace clear minds.

Finally, we must wake up to all of life's illusions
and make a choice, an utterly hard decision.
If, in life, man strives to do what's right,
horror will be far from where it can haunt or bite.

Let your life's window crack wide open.
Let truth's sweet fresh breeze in.
Uplift your soul with sparks of ecstasy.
Rejuvenate, be alive, and jump again.

A Blossom Celebrates the Soul

A gracious smile blossoms on my face.
I am waking up to a new day, strength in me.
Outside, the spring sun graces the horizon.
I am excited. My soul dances to the sweetest tune.

What a wondrous day to wake up to,
anticipating moments I'd be with you.
Time overwhelmingly inches closer,
a profound feeling stirs deep within.

How great it feels to be in your world,
its sweetest essence of belonging.
It fortifies me and my deep inner resolve,
uplifting my soul to however it evolves.

Truly unaware of whatever's lying ahead,
I let the day drag on to whatever comes.
Optimism comforts me in my solitude,
each passing moment feeling good.

Whatever the day brings is beyond me.
I'll marvel at each moment and memory,
not glazing any gesture with pretense,
but rather embracing the day's promise.

I don't know how things will turn out.
I float through each moment without doubt.
Whatever ensues, I see without a clue.
Today my soul is meant to celebrate you.

A Gift

Life—
a breath of love to the dust given
for us to enjoy and take care of,
to treasure and float with its cycle.

Free will—
a gift given to humans at birth,
a tool to set sail on the sea of life.
At a crossroads, it helps one to decide.

Wisdom—
comes with free will,
manifesting a sense of maturity,
the voice lighting the way.

Freedom—
a gift to fight for, to work on,
inalienable for the righteous,
not absolute and cannot be lost.

Love—
a gift from the Life-Giver,
immeasurable and overwhelming,
one to be treasured by a grateful receiver.

Pleasure—
for those who seek,
meaningless if wantonly achieved,
the pure ones thrive eternally for the meek.

Delight—
does not come as easily,
but the pure emanates from within,
inexplicable, a comforting feeling.

A Glimpse of My Future

One early morning after the break of dawn,
she waits with patience for her ride.
Her eyes grow tired and her body weary.
In her, a glimpse of what my life could be.

In one cozy lobby, the fireplace ablaze,
warmth lulling her to a sweet slumber.
Fighting hard against falling back to sleep,
eyes slowly closing as her lids get heavier.

Reaching out, I hold her hands now wrinkly.
She raises her head up, stares at me gently.
Breaking into smile, she manages to whisper:
"Tomorrow at church, we'll worship together."

Smiling wearily, her eyes never leave me.
She surveys my face with the softest smile.
In her eyes, evidence of real fondness for me.
The past emerges in the forefront of her memory.

Squeezing my hand, she utters: "Thank you—
for being here patiently, for not leaving me alone."
Smiling, she asks if I'll be waiting for her
when she comes back later that afternoon.

Staring at her, I see a glimpse of my future,
what it would be like all alone growing old.
In that one brief moment, I murmur to myself:
"Alone, I'd be fearless, for God is my refuge."

A Heart's Intent

With love,
I share with you
blessings I have received.

His love
through your kindness
is manifested in me.

A prayer
comes with this gift,
the prospect of success.

My words
and my promises
come with honor, my only wealth.

A New Leaf Uncurls Preparing for Fall

Be cognizant, always mindful.
Pray for wisdom and be keen.
Shades of truth do seem surreal—
sometimes real, but more often misleading.

So whenever tomorrow comes,
be warned, on constant guard.
Signs so grim might be lurking
on that leaf of life vaguely written.

Tomorrow's a moment to await.
It's a gift that we're quite beholden to,
wrapped up with all of our uncertainties.
Be wary of its dawning.

The power of knowing is within.
It's been with each of us since birth,
affording us the ability to discern
good from bad deeds, to do the right thing.

So if tomorrow comes as a gift
to enjoy as we sojourn on earth,
heed admonitions never to lean
on your own folly of misunderstanding.

As each day unfolds a new leaf,
we are uncertain what's in store.
Anticipate not a moment of ease.
Not all are rainbow-colored days.

As each day unfolds, yes, beware.
Hold on to the truth, our only shield.
For only truth leads, wins battles,
as the new leaves change to crinkle and rattle.

A Year-End Prayer

With bended knees, I pray,
thanking You for the life and strength
You have once again gifted me.
May this very day start blissfully.

My heart implores.
You see how I have heavily rested
my burdens onto You.
Each breath of life is truly a blessing.

As I pray, I cry my heart out.
The old year is ending with deepest pain.
Yet I do anticipate a prosperous new year.
Let blessings pour out from the highest heavens.

I implore at this very moment:
Navigate my path with Your powerful hand.
Take care of my life.
May this year end with an enlightened heart.

Please do not abandon me
as I face life's many worries and strifes.
Please be with me as You always have been.
Make me feel I am Your child.

An Eerie Sense of Foreboding

Life is laced with uncertainties.
Not one person has the power to discern
what the next moment holds.
Risks abound with every inch.

Life is not meant to be bitter.
Since borrowed, it is for all to enjoy.
It has streaks of tricky choices
ostensibly arising as a ploy.

Generally, willpower plays out
when life's tricks present themselves.
Instantly, Lady Wisdom calls—
be safe, listen, heed her dictates.

Truthfully, life's akin to a race.
It's never given without a purpose
that comes with tests or tribulations.
Life's a race quite worthy to begin.

Life's an amazing gift,
a wondrous creation.
We find its joy
when we surmount arising glitches.

That sunset behind the horizon—
like life's race to the finish line.
As one rides off toward the sunset,
proving in life we are blessed.

But life has uncertainties
coming and, because we know not when,
an eerie sense of foreboding
is always on the horizon.

At Day's End

In bed, I sit up in my deep solitude,
looking inside, counting my blessings.
The ones I can only feel lift my spirits.
Grateful, I look up as my heart sings.

Tears of joy pool in my eyes,
grateful I made it through the day.
Doubtless, I knew that Almighty hands
held me tight, guided me on my way.

Though I feel weary, so heavily laden,
a smile still gently blossoms on my face
just remembering at each day's end
to supplicate on bended knees.

The next day I'll face with enthusiasm
coupled with an ounce of determination.
Deep in me, I believe I will surmount
the high mountains of life's confusion

with the strength with which I've been blessed
and the blessings of health and mental sanity.
Of the most vital of moments I can't live without,
being of service is what living is all about.

At each day's end, I beg and beseech
that He sees my heart and reads my mind,
hoping both gifts of knowledge and wisdom
can be wielded to the fullest.

Before My Time

Sixty-nine years and thirteen more days to go.
With God's blessings and gift of life, I'll turn seventy.
I'm looking forward to still being healthy and strong.
Most of all, I'm praying sanity won't leave me yet.

Quietly sitting on a chair, gathering all my thoughts
about what has molded me and what I have become.
Rolling up my sleeves, I tried beating life's odds.
My daily struggles have toughened me up.

Life's challenges piled up at various times before me,
incessantly shaking up my strong resolve.
For one moment in time, a dream so deeply entrenched—
to free my family from lack, to be filled and gratified.

Recalling my parents, siblings were so hard-pressed,
facing daily life's war to survive as underprivileged.
My father, so intent on putting food on all our plates.
My mother, devotedly performing her chores at her best.

Many events of life did come our way.
And many odds we all faced together, patiently,
hoping our misery-filled world would somehow clear up.
On bended knees, we looked up and never stopped.

Being alive and together was a blessing in itself.
What we lacked we made up. Being together was enough.
And my mother, just like a hen to her tender chicks,
would gather us all and make sure we were safe.

School was a huge temptation I failed resisting.
Our lack in life came as a hindrance, but I persisted.
In my tender years, these words endlessly echoed:
"Where there's a will, there's a way," I remembered.

And we all know light always swallows the dark.
The evening falls, but in a few hours comes daylight again.
The sun rises from the farthest east
then sits down beyond the horizon in the west.

What would life be if everything moved in parallel?
All we would see is monotony,
no challenges to set everything in motion.
To what end would life aspire without having a goal?

Treading on roads difficult to cross or walk,
unfazed by my family's lack of privilege,
working for a living in daytime and being a student at night.
Through all righteous means, I rolled up my sleeves.

Thriving on the little that my parents could give,
I saved it all and gave back to them in times of need.
I was satisfied earning ten cents a page typing essays
with my mind focused on finishing college.

I had been lured into coping with life
by indulging heavily in the cigarette smoking
that I can trace back to my grandmother—
when I lit up her tobacco, obeyed, and then again.

Hooked since I was seven, I bought my own cigarettes
which lasted for over twenty-five years of my life.
If not for the fatal illness,
I'd have died of cancer with no one else to blame.

With awe and amazement, I was weaned from it,
remembering nothing that I'd ever taken a puff of.
So when I recouped from thyrotoxic heart disease,
a trachea tube was fitted to help me breathe with ease.

I've been breathing through a metal trachea tube
for thirty-five years and still strong.
Deep in my heart, I know to whom I owe thanks—
the One Almighty God who has preserved my life.

I've not been seriously ill since, not bedridden.
What I am now and what I have become are proof
that not only relying on my own understanding of things,
but also having deep faith, has shaped me into who I am.

Best of Things

Is it fame?
An achievement akin to a pedestal.
Be not oblivious like a flower.
In time, it withers. It's not perpetual.

Is it beauty?
It magnetizes, generally skin-deep.
Learn to discern where real beauty lies—
not what meets the eye, but what's beneath.

Is it wealth?
It amazingly empowers, indulges,
but intangibles it generally cannot buy—
like true love, health, and happiness.

Is it freedom?
One incredible and intricate word,
for it has cost and is never absolute,
a devious idea that's often abused.

Is it intelligence?
One of man's driving forces,
the other knowledge to lord over the world,
oblivious that both are useless down in the grave.

Is it happiness?
An emotion one fakes at times,
but one that also emanates from deep inside—
exuded with bliss, laced with pride.

Is it honesty?
Truly one of the world's rarities.
Many try, not for a show.
Truth comes to light; it can betray you.

Is it kindness?
One thing tougher to do.
It surfaces from deep within.
At random, it shows its real meaning.

Is it friends?
Ones treated as gifts, treasured.
They, unlike acquaintances,
are needed rarities in dire times.

Is it health?
Sometimes people flaunt the body,
not realizing there's more to it.
Health entails the physical and inner spirit.

Is it power?
Lording over the world,
oblivious of the Creator's presence—
the only Source of life, the only Lord.

Is it love?
An emotion sometimes lightly regarded,
when the real one oozes, unconditional.
The source is alive, dwelling, and eternal.

The Hard Choice I Made

There came a time in my life
when various problems hit hard,
piled up on top of each other.
I ended up feeling terribly sad.

The world began to darken.
The walls inched nearer, closing in.
I was perplexed, stupefied,
and failed to hear the voice within.

Bitter tears started pooling,
cascaded without notice.
I tried so hard to wipe them away,
but they would not stop.

My resolve began to weaken,
tempting me to cave in, give up.
Before me were life's hard choices.
I felt tricked, eternally trapped.

Always to the heavens I'd look up
with teary eyes closed tightly.
I'd say the most fervent of my prayers,
asking for wisdom to come swiftly.

Heeding the voice from within:
"To the truth. Try not to lose sight,
for it soothes the troubled soul."
And it lifted my lagging spirits up.

What does it really cause anyone
swimming against life's current?
Where would one's life end up?
Without willpower, nothing plays out.

Wonder not if at times we're pressed
between solid rocks, impossibly tight.
Contemplate and take deep breaths.
Marvel at the beauty of what life truly is.

Discern that life poses a challenge.
No one can run away from nor escape it,
but we're in the world for special reasons.
These hard times are just a season.

Conversing with Nature

Deep in thought, settled on a chair,
I wait for the frail lady I've known.
The lobby entrance door opens and closes.
I exchange hellos with others, never alone.

Fleeting moments of quietude come,
leaving me all to myself.
Amid dead silence, ignoring those passing by,
my eyes feast on the blue summer sky.

Down the road, cars of different makes run to and fro.
Wheelchairs are pushed by loving arms.
Intently watched doors closing and opening
see frail ones held by gentle hands.

In those folks, I see a glimpse of my life.
I could be one in my gray, older days.
I have supplicated, to God I plead.
May His ears to me incline and grant my wishes.

Teary eyes lifted up to the skies,
the perfect sight amazes me to no end.
Seattle's rain and the shoreline
quench the thirst of the evergreens.

Skies are not true-blue at the moment,
but green treetops grace my view,
twigs gently swaying with the wind
as graceful dancers do.

A gentle smile blossoms on my face
as the swaying entertains me.
I feel urged to join them, nudged on.
Too soon beauty fades.

Quietly, I remain seated, still amazed,
my inner voice whispering to feast on the view
before my eyes without wasting a moment.
The sky now shows evident changes.

Cotton balls of white clouds hover,
the beauty of the sky now enhanced
effortlessly by gentle brushstrokes
painted by unseen hands.

The white clouds dissipate
as gentle winds blow them eastward.
I look up with a smile still to the north,
acknowledging the awe in His handiwork.

Enjoying Life's Ride

Life as a gift is never a mystery,
and into this world we all set sail
with gentle hands leading the way—
a mother's heart that wishes us well.

Along the way are learning fields
of grand ideas or useful advice
about things that serve to be our armor
with choices set before our eyes.

The gift of knowledge we are all given.
And wisdom, too, a gift
to hold onto with the greatest of care
to remain afloat and never fear.

Never oblivious that life is a ride—
a roller coaster moving over and down hills—
with challenges before us never ceasing.
Misfortunes befall us without notice.

A phase of life for each to live.
Take to heart every low or high tide,
fully knowing we all have choices
when we realize that life is not a free ride.

Always aware of life's every aspect,
knowing every ride has consequences.
Hasty actions that we make
eternally haunt and make us restless.

He who gave us life is just and faithful.
He set us out to sail with the shields we need.
Using the knowledge and wisdom with which we're gifted
for us all to heed.

Precious gifts we need to treasure,
for they make paths as bright as day
when we stumble through the pitch-darkness.
Within the course, we all can stay.

The pure-hearted warrior fears nothing
through all steep cliffs and hard terrain.
With ease, he swims through life's deepest seas
and surmounts the highest of mountains.

Faith, the Invisible Shield

Life is akin to a war—
ordeals, tests, trials, and enemies.
We are each encouraged to wear a shield,
the kind based on each individual need.

Most of us are brave enough,
have been toughened up to be bold.
Though no one is judged by words uttered,
but by the faith and good deeds they uphold.

Discern that not all actions can be enough,
if one stands alone, frustratingly apart.
For alone each is useless, as it's been written:
faith without work is dead and barren.

They are codependent and intertwined.
Each sheds light when applied together.
It works through faith, a force to reckon with.
To recapitulate, it's both faith and deed.

Friendship and Its Occasional Ambiguities

Remnants of past events still pain me.
In various shapes, they come to haunt.
Sweet words now bitter, still echoing,
following along like a shadow.

Everywhere a deafening whisper
reminding me to never again stumble,
nudging me to keep friendship doors shut,
build a higher, thicker glass wall.

I've been trying to scrap ghosts,
scrubbing imprints off my memory.
Sad memories adhere, they cling—
those disheartening souls I had failed to see.

I must have done some good
because good deeds prevail.
So when clouds of gray hover above,
comforting gestures from true friends abound.

Now hope glimmers over life's horizon.
Unyielding, I stand, resolute and sound,
moving on and worrying about nothing,
in touch with the friends that still abound.

Every speck of life I personally regard
for its truest value and worth.
As any journey begins with a small step,
one simple hello kindles a friendship.

As my world turns this much, I can say:
never ever take a true friend for granted
or forget to show you care.
Each word is an honor or a promise made.

Glorious Scene from the Backyard

Peeking through the dust-tinted glass door,
all over faint green grass. Clearly, I see
rotting leaves spread over the backyard,
the colors contrasted into a pleasant view.

A garden now bare as the season changes.
Green leafy plants vanish from sight.
Lean stalks of mustard still manifesting,
some few days back were proudly green.

Few trees have lost their vibrant glow,
bare twigs enduring the snow.
Succumbing to change
feels so helpless whenever the winds blow.

Along barbed wires are flowering plants.
Sturdy roots of grapevine still visible,
seemingly dead like rocks barely buried,
soon will be budding, undead.

Above me appear thick clouds of gray,
hovering motionless. The skies look grim.
I stare at them. They're mirroring my feelings—
tears now pooling and sadness manifesting.

Deep in my heart, a spirit heavily laden
with tests, trials, and a few of life's burdens.
The stillness of the moment is quite numbing.
The quietness, deafening.

For signs I hope to find through the motion of leaves,
likewise from those leafless twigs.
I see motion in the pale green backyard.
Witnessing this sight lights up my soul.

Yes. Come, gentle motion and rustling sounds.
Leaves are crawling, inching on the ground.
Along the fence, green leaves now sway
and vibrant twigs dance in the wind.

From my eyes where hot tears begin cascading,
a new sensation goes up and down my spine.
For all that I see, a life is manifesting
from an almost-dead backyard scene.

Life has its bizarre way of changing us
like the glorious scene before my very eyes.
A power in the backyard shows
me a reassuring presence and my spirits glow.

How Our Friendship Came to Be

I remember the night we first talked.
Fingers of fate must have made us abide,
for while you were quietly sat in a chair,
a gentle force nudged me to your side.

Exchanging greetings with decent smiles,
I said: "Been thinking about you lately."
Politely, you shared with such honesty
that you had also been thinking of me.

Contemplating later over what transpired,
it rendered me truly excited,
for never had I in the least anticipated
such a heart-fulfilling moment coming my way.

In the wake of a friendship evolving,
the ensuing test already lurked in the dark.
You were soon leaving to move far away—
that distance a test to our friendship.

I noticed an exciting turn of events,
bonds tightening with each passing moment,
hoping nothing would change while you were away.
If something did, then I'd let it be.

And you promised nothing would.
My world flickered with hopes renewed.
Happy, I managed one deep sigh of relief
and fully trusted the sincerity of your word.

As always, hope was a motivating factor.
Not all of life is grueling pain.
Wisdom doesn't sketch life as easy.
Friends do make it worth living when they remain.

I Hear You in Silence

Amidst deep silence,
In bed, I intently listen to You, Lord.
Lying awake uttering a solemn prayer,
I seek guidance, refuge.

The day before tonight was long.
I was trying to cope with the busyness of life,
with the dangers You have delivered me,
leaving in Your hands all of my strife.

Driving here or there along life's path
to the various places You took me,
taking to heart and listening to wisdom
is the path I take alongside You.

Alone, things would have been harder—
everything a challenge to surpass.
But when You're with me, my soul is inspired.
You nudge me on, encourage me to never grow tired.

To the right places You have always led me.
Through words of wisdom, I follow.
With strong determination and enthusiasm,
I do the work You intend me to do.

Not for me to either demand or dictate
because it is never my place.
Mine is to obey, serve, and worship;
try to be worthy, sincerely obedient.

Amidst the quietness in my room,
the pitch-darkness and solitude,
I pray to You and beg for various things.
Please pour upon me those blessings.

Living life is not without trials, ordeals,
those tests of faith I have lived through.
You can fathom the very core of my heart.
I need You, Lord! Take me by the hand.

I hear You through the air that I breathe,
in the rhythm of my heartbeat,
through each and every motion made.
In silence even, I hear You lulling me to sleep.

Just Empty Words

Never had I spoiled a man
in any way that I should,
but once in life I trusted
and was misled.

No reason for me to celebrate,
never a drumroll anywhere.
My heart has been seized
in complete fear of falling in love again.

Stupefied, downtrodden,
and too frozen to change direction.
Fear can be devastating,
like losing ground in a battle.

The memory of the touch—
gentle but laced with unfaithfulness,
with bitter feelings deep in my heart—
lost its sweetness and essence.

The moment before the kiss
devilish and quite daunting,
my face burned like a flame.
My deepest anger resurfaced.

All words uttered were empty,
promises made but unkept.
Since then, I've seen nothing but shade—
no hint of a future glowing.

No phones for souls to connect,
nothing to watch and look upon.
I no longer expect you to reappear
before me.

It's too unfortunate that cunning souls
breeze through our lives.
We trust our hearts to them,
only to be left deeply broken.

Soon they become just a part of memory,
the most bitter ones stewing deep within.
And just like the darkest of shadows,
they cannot be gotten rid of or shaken off.

Souls wishing for an endless night
just to rebuild a broken dream,
to gather all stars with the moon,
hoping dawn won't come too soon.

Just Keep Breathing

Life has its ups and downs
much like storms—
those meant to pose some challenge,
make sense of our existence.

Likewise we give meaning to life,
glaze it with rainbow colors.
For downtime comes naturally,
unfazed. We just keep breathing.

Whatever in life comes or goes—
in a flash appearing and disappearing—
it astounds us, shakes our life,
rendering us dizzy or drowning.

Be ready for emotional storms
and the consequences of what we do.
Let's not simply shrug shoulders,
asserting: "No one cares!"

For deep inside screams a voice
on this dazing roller coaster ride.
Feelings we'll never know to be as sweet.
There's so much life in every heartbeat.

Boldly let feelings out in the open.
No matter what, keep on breathing.
Deep feelings should be let out with restraint
instead of doubt.

Feelings are sometimes laced with ambiguity
and letting them out spells trouble,
especially when we are unsure how they might be construed
and form a storm—a whirling feud.

In these instances, fear overwhelms me.
I get lost in how to swallow it back,
conceal the tinge of bitter regret,
averting the monster feelings I create.

Yes, I fear letting them out—
fear of rejection
hovering like dark clouds that loom
breathless amid emotional storms.

The Invisible Wedge

Each person is born with special gifts.
God-willed, brought by fate.
Events shape each passing moment,
a road map to follow with noble intent.

Life presents in unique fashion
as moments unfold.
Good deeds are rarely acknowledged
and acts of kindness are ignored.

We are born to this world with the gifts
of free will and common sense
for all to discern what's right from wrong.
Lady Wisdom, in faith, makes us strong.

Word, wedge, and wisdom are our anchors in life.
Without them, we're lost in bottomless darkness.
Pure words of God we value and take to heart.
When His love enfolds us, our spirit rises.

Temptation has once weakened my resolve.
At a tender age, doors were open to explore.
Cutting classes, at the movies we hung out.
I fully owned up to it and deeply regretted it.

Awakened in awe by the power of atonement,
before me were choices and second chances.
Distraught and alarmed, I left in utter confusion,
lost in sorrow and crying for divine intervention.

Words in riddle I heard and struggled to discern.
Scriptural verses resonated in my ears.
His words, like a wedge, pierced my very core.
In my heart, they adhere. I now hold them dear.

Words like a wedge, my strength, or an anchor.
Only with His words could I move forward.
Bravely facing my tests and trials, unfazed,
I have inched forward and onward.

Life without the wedge would be perilous.
I'd have drifted away.
His words I imbed in my heart,
empowering me to hang on, to not be led astray.

Inspired by His words, feeling enthusiastic,
my friends profess I've been their little wedge.
Meeting confused souls at a crossroads,
looking for guidance and a hand to hold.

Time passed swiftly by and, like fruit, I ripened.
To me, friends reach out when daunted and troubled,
although unaware of the grand scheme of things.
But as a handy wedge, to the occasion I rise.

But why me?
Knowing I could hardly stand on my own,
undeserving of even a second look,
rendered useless with no material possessions.

I was devoid of material wealth.
What one sees of me, I am—
something I wouldn't consider unfortunate
on any given day, my soul in joy would shout.

Most people think alike for many reasons.
They see power through what one possesses.
Harsh, deliberately dismissing the golden rule.
It's what meets the eye, not what the heart can fathom.

Does someone's perception of life even matter?
Is the mundane more significant than the heavenly?
Discount neither the wedge nor words of wisdom.
Your shield from the worst has yet to come.

Do not doubt the power of the Invisible Wedge,
the Protector, Mighty Refuge, Life-Giver.
When an enemy approaches like a raging storm,
call, supplicate. He will be there.

Let the Wedge be the anchor in your life's journey,
a guiding light beaming along your horizon.
Appreciate the gift of life no matter how dismal.
God, the Invisible Wedge, rewards life eternal.

Staying Afloat

One grayish morning greeted me
with an air of hope and excitement,
but also with a sense of eerie quietness
in the stillness of the moment.

The eastern horizon showed no signs of daylight,
no visible golden rays of the sun.
But behind those blankets of gray clouds,
I knew the sun was smiling without a doubt.

For a moment, I paused to ponder
what the day would bring.
Determined to stay afloat,
I would patiently row my own life's boat.

In Him, I left my life and strength
as I set sail for my day's adventure,
aware of no other safe refuge
but under His wings, I'm sure.

Onward I rowed my boat through
the changing tides of life,
riding the waves even as they got rough
and a little threatening.

Deep within, my fear stirred,
aware of the day's uncertainties.
Wavering faith is what would defeat me.
I needed strength to fight rough waters.

While sanity dictates the logical
and the heart debates with reason,
wisdom speaks through the heart—
it's a small voice with a guiding light.

Life is so much like the sea.
Its depth we discern with special care.
The sea is filled with threats,
dangers abounding far beneath.

Discern tiny signals of the tides
and where the current flows.
Don't row against obvious ripples,
for they might not bring you back ashore.

Keeping a Dream Alive

Through my mind's window
I peek, rewinding events,
the briefest of recollections,
memories of my farthest past.

I see scenes of an innocent soul
aspiring, building a dream
at a time when dreams were wishes.
Tearfully, I muster a grin.

Strangely, the dream of writing poems remains
and has been imprinted on my core.
Though at some point forgotten,
it's now deeply secured even more.

Events would push it to the foreground
as streaks of anguish played out.
The dream always finds its way back,
rewinds to remind me what it's about.

Dreams are just dreams, as they say.
In time, they diminish
like overly ripe fruits of wishful thinking,
falling to nothing,

just like the vast blue seas yonder,
shifting with the changing tides.
And so like our very own existence
that's forgotten the moment we die.

Manifesting unchanging routines,
repeating at every moment's call.
Tides recede and obviously rise,
contributing to the ocean's natural cycle.

But nature's cycle is far different
from how human nature works.
As time passes, some things
don't diminish, but instead fully develop.

I rewind my life's events in decades
and reflect on how the dream began.
In the back mirror of a youthful mind,
one unflattering moment in time.

The painful sight of poverty and need
struck my life at a tender age.
If only to alleviate my family's problems,
I hoped for the best and dared to dream.

My heart still dreams, hanging on,
still squeezing through against the odds.
Patiently, I swim towards the horizon
hoping the blessings pour forth soon.

Time passes me by,
childhood dreams still elusive.
Supplicating, may God incline His ears
and send the blessings I deserve.

Reshaping a Heart

Life has had me travel countless miles.
I used up all the means I've had on hand.
Be it in print or imaginary, I've taken steps.
Dreams have had me roll through various lands.

I've feasted on nature's awesome scenes,
communed with God's magnificent work.
I've exchanged smiles with perfect strangers
and shaken hands with some along the road.

Friends have come and gone as my world turned.
I've met new ones in some diverse situations   .
The gift of love that I carry with me
has been challenged beyond imagination.

I fearlessly leave it all to the heavens,
ever seeking protection to shelter me.
Shield me from those with evil intent,
those who are treacherous or my faith's enemy.

I'm quite mindful of every word I've uttered,
so I'd be spoken to in return just as I expect.
With pure intent of doing the right thing,
I try to be gracious and think ahead.

I know every action has a reaction
that could be both serious and profound.
Little missteps could've dug me deeper,
but I did not spiral down.

In my solitude, in the deepest supplication,
I ask for sound psyche and inner peace.
I ask to be a friend to all and no one's enemy.
I aim to sow kindness.

At some point along the road, love seized me.
I trusted and had been trusted in return.
Relationships crept into my life,
hoping they would last and never end.

Days passed swiftly; years rolled along.
Heavenly hands nudged me to and from places.
In all of my life's rolling,
I ended up in the awesome city of Shoreline.

As a square peg, I fit into a square hole,
smoothing rough edges to suit a need,
adjusting things to fit into this new world.
I work, conserve, and feed myself so I'll live.

The years I've lived were my best teachers.
I've learned lessons from lack and poverty.
Every fiber of my being has been touched.
Happiness found in all things has reshaped my heart.

Love helped me attain what I doubted inside,
as did friendship and mutual understanding—
something profound, deep, so unaffected.
I have been gently guided by the hands of the heavens.

By seizing, nurturing, and letting them grow,
tokens of love I had treasured freely flowed.
Without this love, my life and existence
would be hollow.

A New Year, a New Phase

Like a book, God flips life's page
and a moment's event presents itself,
one I deeply hope for
in utter amazement, not a daze.

A glimpse of hope, of cherished dreams
is manifesting more favorably.
I supplicate for heavenly blessings
with no expectation they'll come pouring.

Heartily probing what's on each page,
I find a lot more than I ever thought,
some in passing fancy.
Fervent prayers are never for naught.

Cognizant of what to live for,
struggling each day to survive
with full reliance on Divine Providence,
I want to receive what I richly deserve.

Willingly, I march onward each day
with thoughts not only of myself.
I'm determined to share what little I have
with souls who need it just as much.

Whatever is written on each page of life,
I willingly heed to in time.
Gladly welcoming guidelines served
through Lady Wisdom, I toe the line.

God reads my mind and my heart,
all that I think of and what I'm feeling.
I pray He does not hold them against me,
for I am weak and in need of strengthening.

As a new phase of life swiftly approaches,
something so beyond what we can hold,
I bend my knees in fervent prayer.
"Hear me, O Lord, as You always do.

Help me, I pray, to carry my yoke
with a solemn promise of serving You!
Please lead me to the certain path where I should go,
lending me wisdom to ever be righteous."

Hope Comes Back Flickering

Rising, a spark of hope comes flickering,
after being faded and waned.
A glimmer of hope, no matter how tiny,
is a sign conveyed quite clearly.

Enthused, I've since started dreaming
of seeing you reach your life's goal.
Sadly, the only thing I can offer
is the whisper of a fervent prayer.

Confidently, I see you at the apex
standing with pride, humility, and grace—
a reward attained in a sensible balance.
You deserve heaven-sent success.

Inspired, I pledge solemnly to lend a hand,
willing to do things you'd much prefer.
Self-reliance does make you prouder.
The success feels enormously sweeter.

Just notice how each spark gets brighter.
Even horizons get a lot clearer.
Know by heart that a dream is in God's hands
and materializes only in His own time.

Circumstances eventually change as they do.
We know nothing really stays forever.
In time, I'll slowly take my grandest exit,
leaving memories for you to remember.

Again, let me share with you words of wisdom:
Never give up if I am laid to rest and gone.
Never draw or step back even an inch,
for hope does always come back flickering.

Lighten Up and Fly

The world as we see it
dimming before our eyes.
Unsure of who to blame,
can't even point a finger.

No one ever wishes
for a hard life.
Men expect and desire
easier paths to tread.

Somehow, against wishes,
situations happen as they do.
No man can bring back time.
The world keeps turning ahead.

One truth we must remember
is the purpose of His creation:
He, the One True God,
and we, His people.

He who created everything
with humankind in mind.
He who warned of travails ahead.
He who set specific guidelines.

He didn't mean for man to suffer.
He loves all of His creations
and provides us with what we need.
The deserving ones surely receive.

Take His words to heart.
His guidelines are easy,
for with them comes His love.
He expects humanity to obey.

Are all hardships before us
burdensome? No, not at all,
for He has given man the wisdom to persist.
Unload your yoke in prayer.

He listens to fervent prayer,
so seek out His guidance
through the pages of the Scriptures
and seek some more.

Stand in the shade of His wings.
Rely on Divine Providence.
Life can be easier to live
under His wings. Chill out and fly.

A Gift of Spring

Patches of gray clouds hover.
Like a painting, they're incredibly still.
Skies like a canvas awaiting acrylic,
orange sunrays bursting through the clouds.

Trees point upward and stand still,
deep green leaves reflecting over this work of art
like hands raised up or hearts reaching out
to the highest of heavens.

Outside, the air seems crisp, chilly.
Bathing the earth in light, a glimpse of spring.
Lingering winter winds softly exit
until they are just a memory.

Today unfolds the first page of another season:
Flowers have sprung.
From nodes of twigs, buds emerge.
When they bloom, breathtaking sights abound.

As the minutes roll on towards warm midday,
my thoughts fast-forward towards day's end.
Time is always rolling forward, never stopping for us.
Regardless of time, I've always kept you close.

I peek through a window and lean on the sill.
You come to mind with your gentle smile,
reflecting on white canvas over gray skies.
Deep in me, I wish my heart no longer cried.

Today a little bud of hope begins to spring.
In harmony, it appears with the new season.
Within that hope, love thrives, waiting to be realized
in a special moment I'll quietly feast upon.

You opened your world and let me in—
a world so exclusive not a soul could enter.
Just like a painter, you hold tight to your brush,
choosing only select images to perk up your canvas.

Today is the moment you've long awaited.
With pride, raise up the torch you have earned,
as your heart shines upon all whom you love.
The speck you'll share with me, I'll gladly receive.

Graciously, I thank you for making me a part
of finishing college, a significant moment in your life.
Whatever I've done, I seek nothing in return.
My hopes for your successes persist to burn.

Today presents your life's deeper meaning.
I'll always be close behind.
In this special moment, may your heart sing.
I bring you the gift of love and the warm hope of spring.

Love and Its Power

Every soul that falls for love
is possessed, enslaved
by this powerful emotion.
Man has always been bewitched.

My heart is deeply pained
with one sting to the bone.
Its torment reaches to the core.
In prayer, I ask for help and more.

But love and its power,
like huge magnets,
have a penchant to pull on us.
The soul floats with this motion.

It's a pull toward someone
and, like gravity, no heart can resist.
We lose the willpower to resist
at the moment we least expect.

It never takes that long
for a soul that's clearly fallen
to swallow up bitter pride
when rules of faithfulness have been broken.

Love holds without touching,
promising a soul to hang on without committing.
And a soul that drowns in love
will later wallow in pain.

Amidst moments of deep pain,
the soul seeks calm and steady love,
to be set free
from past mistakes.

I have tried resisting love's magnet.
I have even forced my heart to stone.
I have determined to never give up
with reasons quite simple and known.

But how could one ever resist
such an overwhelming feeling?
Attempting to stand my ground against love
is a futile effort.

Somehow in moments of solitude
with knees bent, we find love's knack.
The heart always knows
love finds its own way back.